WASHINGTON AND THE PRINCIPLES OF THE REVOLUTION:

AN

ORATION

DELIVERED BEFORE THE

MUNICIPAL AUTHORITIES OF THE CITY OF BOSTON,

AT THE CELEBRATION OF

The Declaration of American Independence,

JULY 4, 1850.

BY EDWIN P. WHIPPLE.

SECOND EDITION.

BOSTON:
TICKNOR, REED, AND FIELDS.
M.DCCC.L.

BOSTON:
PRINTED BY JOHN WILSON,
21, School Street.

CITY OF BOSTON.

IN THE BOARD OF MAYOR AND ALDERMEN,
Monday, July 8, 1850.

It was unanimously

Voted, That the thanks of the City Council be presented to EDWIN P. WHIPPLE, Esquire, for the very able, eloquent, and appropriate Oration delivered by him, before the Municipal Authorities of the City, at their recent celebration of the Anniversary of the Declaration of American Independence; and especially, for his bold, discriminating, and just analysis of the Character of Washington.

Voted, That he be requested to furnish a copy of the said Oration for publication.

Sent down for concurrence.

JOHN P. BIGELOW, *Mayor.*

IN COMMON COUNCIL, JULY 11, 1850.

Read and concurred.

FRANCIS BRINLEY, *President.*

A true copy.

Attest: S. F. M'CLEARY, *City Clerk.*

ORATION.

The day, Gentlemen, we have here met to commemorate, in the spirit of a somewhat soberer joy than rings in the noisy jubilee of the streets, is not a day dedicated to liberty in the abstract, but a day especially consecrated to American liberty and American independence. The true character of that liberty is to be sought in the events of our colonial history, in the manners and laws of our colonial forefathers, and, above all, in the stern, brief epitome of our whole colonial life contained in that memorable Declaration, the maxims of whose sturdy wisdom still sound in our ears and linger in our hearts, as we have heard them read in this hall to-day; a Declaration peculiar among all others of its kind, not merely for the fearless free spirit which beats and burns beneath every decisive sentence, but from its combination of clearness in the statement of particular grievances with audacity in the announcement of general principles; a Declaration, indeed, abounding in sentiments of liberty so sinewy and bold, and ideas of liberty so exact and practical, that it bears on every immortal feature the signs of representing a people, to whom liberty had been long familiar as a living law, as an organized institution, as a homely, household fact. The peculiarities which distinguish the whole substance and tone of this solemn instrument are peculiarities of the American revolution itself, giving dignity to its events and import to its principles, as they gave success to its arms.

Liberty, considered as an element of human nature, would naturally, if unchecked, follow an ideal law of development, appearing first as a dim but potent sentiment; then as an intelligent sentiment, or idea; then as an organized idea, or body of institutions, recognizing mutual rights and enforcing mutual duties. But, in its historical development, we find that the unselfish nature of liberty is strangely intermixed with its selfish perversion; that, in struggling with outward oppression, it develops inward hatreds; that the sentiment is apt to fester into a malignant passion, the idea to dwindle into a barren opinion, and this passionate opinion to issue in anarchy, which is despotism disorganized, but as selfish, wolfish, and ravenous under its thousand wills as under its one. These hostile elements, which make up the complex historical fact of liberty, — one positive, the other negative, — one organizing, the other destructive, — are always at work in human affairs with beneficent or baleful energy; but, as society advances, the baser elements give way by degrees to the nobler, and liberty ever tends to realize itself in law. The most genial operation of its creative spirit is when it appears as a still, mysterious, plastic influence, silently and surely modifying the whole constitution of a despotic society, stealing noiselessly into manners, insinuating itself into the administration of laws, grafting new shoots upon the decaying trunks of old institutions, and insensibly building up in a people's mind a character strong enough to maintain rights which are also customs. If its most beneficent influence be seen in its gradual organization of liberties, of sentiments rooted in facts, its most barren effect for good is when it scatters abstract opinions of freedom, true to nothing existing in a people's practical life, and scorning all alliance with manners or compromise with fact. This is a fertile source of disorder, of revolts which end in massacres, of Ages of Reason which end in Reigns of Terror; and perhaps the failure of most of the European movements comes from their being either mad uprisings against the pressure of intolerable miseries, or fruitless strivings to establish abstract principles. Such principles, however excellent as propositions, can influence only a small minority of a nation, for a nation rises only in defence of rights which have been violated, not for rights which it has never exerçised; and abstract "liberty, equality, and fraternity," pushed by amiable sentimentalists like Lamartine, and Satanic sentimentalists like Ledru Rollin, have found their fit result in the armed bureau-ocracy, now encamped in Paris, under the ironical nickname of "French Republic."

Now, it was the peculiar felicity of our position, that free institutions were planted here at the original settlement of the country, —

institutions which De Tocqueville considers founded on principles far in advance of the wisest political science of Europe at that day; and accordingly our revolution began in the defence of rights which were customs, of ideas which were facts, of liberties which were laws; and these rights, ideas, and liberties, embodying as they did the common life and experience of the people, were truly considered a palpable property, an inalienable inheritance of freedom, which the Stamp Act, and the other measures of colonial taxation, threatened with confiscation. Parliament, therefore, appeared in America as a spoiler, making war upon the people it assumed to govern, and it thus stimulated and combined the opposition of all classes; for a wrong cannot but be universally perceived when it is universally felt. By thus starting up in defence of the freedom they really possessed, the colonies vastly increased it. In struggling against innovation, they "innovated" themselves into independence; in battling against novelties, they wrought out into actual form the startling novelty of constitutional American liberty. It was because they had exercised rights that they were such proficients in principles; it was because they had known liberty as an institution that they understood it as a science.

Thus it was not the perception of abstract opinions, but the inspiration of positive institutions, which gave our forefathers the heart to brave, and the ability successfully to defy, the colossal power of England; but it must be admitted that in its obnoxious colonial policy England had parted with her wisdom, and in parting with her wisdom had weakened her power; falling, as Burke says, under the operation of that immutable law "which decrees vexation to violence, and poverty to rapine." The England arrayed against us was not the England, which, a few years before, its energies wielded by the lofty and impassioned genius of the elder Pitt, had smitten the power and humbled the pride of two great European monarchies, and spread its fleets and armies, animated by one vehement soul, over three quarters of the globe. The administrations of the English government, from 1760 to the close of our revolutionary war, were more or less directed by the intriguing incapacity of the king. George the Third is said to have possessed many private virtues, — and very private for a long time he kept them from his subjects, — but, as a monarch, he was without magnanimity in his sentiments, or enlargement in his ideas; prejudiced, uncultivated, bigoted, and perverse; and his boasted morality and piety, when exercised in the sphere of government, partook of the narrowness of his mind and the obstinacy of his will; his conscience being used to transmute his hatreds into duties, and his religious sentiment to sanctify his vindictive passions; and as it was his ambition to rule an empire by the petty politics of a court, he preferred rather to have his folly flattered by parasites than his ignorance enlightened by statesmen. Such a disposition in the king of a free country was incompatible with efficiency in the conduct of affairs, as it split parties into factions, and made established principles yield to mean personal expedients. Bute, the king's first minister, after a short administration unexampled for corruption and feebleness, gave way before a storm of popular contempt and hatred. To him succeeded George Grenville, the originator of the Stamp Act, and the blundering promoter of American independence. Grenville was a hard, sullen, dogmatic, penurious man of affairs, with a complete mastery of the details of parliamentary business, and threading with ease all the labyrinths of English law, but limited in his conceptions, fixed in his opinions, without any of that sagacity which reads results in their principles, and chiefly distinguished for a kind of sour honesty, not infrequently found in men of harsh tempers and technical intellects. It was soon discovered, that though imperious enough to be a tyrant he was not servile enough to be a tool; that the same domineering temper which enabled him to push arbitrary measures in Parliament, made him put insolent questions in the palace; and the king, in despair of a servant who could not tax America and persecute Wilkes, without at the same time insulting his master, dismissed him for the Marquis of Rockingham, the leader of the great Whig connection, and a sturdy friend of the Americans both before the revolution and during its progress. Under him the Stamp Act was repealed; but his administration soon proved too liberal to satisfy the fawning politicians who governed the understanding of the king; and the experiment was tried of a composite ministry, put together by Chatham, consisting of members selected from different factions, but without any principle of cohesion to unite them; and the anarchy inherent in the arrangement became portentously apparent, when Chatham, driven by the gout into a state of nervous imbecility, left it to work out its mission of misrule, and its eccentric control was seized by the Chancellor of the Exchequer, the gay, false, dissipated, veering, presumptuous, and unscrupulous Charles Townsend. This man was so brilliant and fascinating as an orator, that Walpole said of one of his speeches, that it was like hearing Garrick act extempore scenes from Congreve; but he was without any guiding moral or political principles; and, boundlessly admired by the House of Commons and boundlessly craving its admiration, he seemed to act ever from the impulses of vanity, and speak ever from the inspiration of champagne. Grenville, smarting under his recent defeat, but still doggedly bent on having a revenue raised in America, missed no opportunity of goading this versatile political *roué* with his sullen and bitter sarcasms. "You are cowards," said he on one occasion, turning to the Treasury bench; "you are afraid of the Americans; you dare not tax America." Townsend, stung by this taunt, started passionately up from his seat, exclaiming, "Fear! cowards! dare not tax America! I do dare tax America!" and this boyish bravado ushered in the celebrated bill, which was to cost England thirteen colonies, add a hundred millions of pounds to her debt, and affix an ineffaceable stain on her public character. Townsend, by the grace of a putrid fever, was saved from witnessing the consequences of his vainglorious presumption; and the direction of his policy eventually fell into the hands of Lord North, a good-natured, second-rate, jobbing statesman, equally destitute of lofty virtues and splendid vices, under whose administration the American war was commenced and consummated. Of all the ministers of George the Third, North was the most esteemed by his sovereign; for he had the tact to follow plans which originated in the king's unreasoning brain and wilful disposition, and yet to veil their weak injustice in a drapery of arguments furnished from his own more enlarged mind and easier temper. Chatham and Camden thundered against him in the Lords; Burke and Fox, Cassandras of ominous and eloquent prophecy, raved and shouted statesmanship to him in the Commons, and screamed out the maxims of wisdom in ecstasies of invective; but he, good-naturedly tolerant to political adversaries, blandly indifferent to popular execration, and sleeping quietly through whole hours of philippics hot with threats of impeachment, pursued his course of court-ordained folly with the serene composure of an Ulysses or a Somers. The war, as conducted by his ministry, was badly managed; but he had one wise thought which happily failed to become a fact. The command in America, on the breaking out of serious disturbances, was offered to Lord Clive; but, fortunately for us, Clive, at about that time, concluded to commit suicide, and our rustic soldiery were thus saved from meeting in the field a general, who, in vigor of will and fertility of resource, was unequalled by any European commander that had appeared since the death of Marlborough. It may here be added, that Lord North's plans of conciliation were the amiabilities of tyranny and benignities of extortion. They bring to mind the little French fable, wherein a farmer convokes the tenants of his barnyard, and with sweet solemnity says, — "Dear animals, I have assembled you here to advise me what sauce I shall cook you with."

"But," exclaims an insurrectionary chicken, "we don't want to be eaten at all!"—to which the urbane chairman replies,—"My child, you wander from the point!"

Such was the government whose policy and whose arms were directed against our rights and liberties during the revolutionary war. As soon as the struggle commenced, it was obvious that England could hold dominion over no portion of the country, except what her armies occupied or wasted for the time; and that the issue of the contest turned on the question as to which would give out first, the obstinacy of the king or the fortitude of the Americans. It was plain that George the Third would never yield except under compulsion from the other forces of the English constitution; that, as long as a corrupt House of Commons would vote supplies, he would prosecute the war, at whatever expense of blood and treasure to England, at whatever infliction of misery upon America. Conquest was hopeless; and Lord North, before the war was half concluded, was in favor of abandoning it; but all considerations of policy and humanity were lost upon the small mind and conscientiously malignant temper of the king. The peculiarity of our struggle consisted in its being with an unwise ruler, who could not understand that war, waged after the objects for which it was declared have utterly failed, becomes mere rapine and murder; and our energy and endurance were put to this terrible test, of bearing up against the king's armies, until the English nation, humbling its irritated pride, should be roused in our behalf, and break down the king's stubborn purpose. We all know, and may we never forget, that this resistance to tyrannical innovation was no fiery outbreak of popular passion, spending itself in two or three battles, and then subsiding into gloomy apathy; but a fixed and reasonable resolve rooted in character, and proof against corrupt and sophistical plans of conciliation, against defeats and massacres, against universal bankruptcy and commercial ruin, — a resolve, which the sight of burning villages and cities turned into British camps, only maddened into fiercer persistence, and which the slow consuming fever of an eight years' war, with its soul-sickening calamities and vicissitudes, could not weaken into submission. The history, so sad and so glorious, which chronicles the stern struggle in which our rights and liberties passed through the awful baptism of fire and blood, is eloquent with the deeds of many patriots, warriors, and statesmen; but these all fall into relations to one prominent and commanding figure, towering up above the whole group in unapproachable majesty, whose exalted character, warm and bright with every public and private virtue, and vital with the essential spirit of wisdom, has burst all sectional and national bounds, and made the name of Washington the property of all mankind.

This illustrious man, at once the world's admiration and enigma, we are taught by a fine instinct to venerate, and by a wrong opinion to misjudge. The might of his character has taken strong hold upon the feelings of great masses of men; but, in translating this universal sentiment into an intelligent form, the intellectual element of his wonderful nature is as much depressed as the moral element is exalted, and consequently we are apt to misunderstand both. Mediocrity has a bad trick of idealizing itself in eulogizing him, and drags him down to its own low level while assuming to lift him to the skies. How many times have we been told that he was not a man of genius, but a person of "excellent common sense," of "admirable judgment," of "rare virtues"! and, by a constant repetition of this odious cant, we have nearly succeeded in divorcing comprehension from his sense, insight from his judgment, force from his virtues, and life from the man. Accordingly, in the panegyric of cold spirits, Washington disappears in a cloud of commonplaces; in the rhodomontade of boiling patriots, he expires in the agonies of rant. Now, the sooner this bundle of mediocre talents and moral qualities, which its contrivers have the audacity to call George Washington, is hissed out of existence, the better it will be for the cause of talent and the cause of morals: contempt of that is the beginning of wisdom. He had no genius, it seems. O no! genius, we must suppose, is the peculiar and shining attribute of some orator, whose tongue can spout patriotic speeches, or some versifier, whose muse can "Hail Columbia," but not of the man who supported states on his arm, and carried America in his brain.

The madcap Charles Townsend, the motion of whose pyrotechnic mind was like the whiz of a hundred rockets, is a man of genius; but George Washington, raised up above the level of even eminent statesmen, and with a nature moving with the still and orderly celerity of a planet round its sun, — he dwindles, in comparison, into a kind of angelic dunce! What is genius? Is it worth any thing? Is splendid folly the measure of its inspiration? Is wisdom its base and summit, — that which it recedes from, or tends towards? And by what definition do you award the name to the creator of an epic, and deny it to the creator of a country? On what principle is it to be lavished on him who sculptures in perishing marble the image of possible excellence, and withheld from him who built up in himself a transcendent character, indestructible as the obligations of Duty, and beautiful as her rewards?

Indeed, if by the genius of action you mean will enlightened by intelligence, and intelligence energized by will, — if force and insight be its characteristics, and influence its test, — and, especially, if great effects suppose a cause proportionably great, that is, a vital causative mind, — then is Washington most assuredly a man of genius, and one whom no other American has equalled in the power of working morally and mentally on other minds. His genius, it is true, was of a peculiar kind, the genius of character, of thought and the objects of thought solidified and concentrated into active faculty. He belongs to that rare class of men, — rare as Homers and Miltons, rare as Platos and Newtons, — who have impressed their characters upon nations without pampering national vices. Such men have natures broad enough to include all the facts of a people's practical life, and deep enough to discern the spiritual laws which underlie, animate, and govern those facts. Washington, in short, had that greatness of character which is the highest expression and last result of greatness of mind; for there is no method of building up character except through mind. Indeed, character like his is not *built* up, stone upon stone, precept upon precept, but *grows* up, through an actual contact of thought with things, — the assimilative mind transmuting the impalpable but potent spirit of public sentiment, and the life of visible facts, and the power of spiritual laws, into individual life and power, so that their mighty energies put on personality, as it were, and act through one centralizing human will. This process may not, if you please, make the great philosopher or the great poet; but it does make the great *man*, — the man in whom thought and judgment seem identical with volition, — the man whose vital expression is not in words, but deeds, — the man whose sublime ideas issue necessarily in sublime acts, not in sublime art. It was because Washington's character was thus composed of the inmost substance and power of facts and principles, that men instinctively felt the perfect reality of his comprehensive manhood. This reality enforced universal respect, married strength to repose, and threw into his face that commanding majesty, which made men of the speculative audacity of Jefferson, and the lucid genius of Hamilton, recognize, with unwonted meekness, his awful superiority.

But, you may say, how does this account for Washington's virtues? Was his disinterestedness will? Was his patriotism intelligence? Was his morality genius? These questions I should answer with an emphatic yes; for there are few falser fallacies than that which represents moral conduct as flowing from moral opinions detached from moral character. Why, there is hardly a tyrant, sycophant, demagogue, or liberticide mentioned in history, who had not enough moral opinions to suffice for a new Eden; and Shakspeare, the sure-seeing poet of human nature, delights to put the most edifying maxims of ethics into the mouths of his greatest villains, of Angelo, of Richard the Third, of the uncle-father of Hamlet. Without doubt Cæsar and Napoleon could have discoursed more fluently than Washington on patriotism, as there are a thousand French republicans, of the last hour's coinage, who could prattle more eloquently than he on freedom. But Washington's morality was built up in warring with outward temptations and inward passions, and every grace of his conscience was a trophy of toil and struggle. He had no moral opinions which hard experience and sturdy discipline had not vitalized into moral sentiments and organized into moral powers; and these powers, fixed and seated in the inmost heart of his character, were mighty and far-sighted forces, which made his intelligence moral and his morality intelligent, and which no sorcery of the selfish passions could overcome or deceive. In the sublime metaphysics of the New Testament, his eye was single, and this made his whole body full of *light.* It is just here that so many other eminent men of action, who have been tried by strong temptations, have miserably failed. Blinded by pride, or whirled on by wrath, they have ceased to discern and regard the inexorable moral laws, obedience to which is the condition of all permanent success; and, in the labyrinths of fraud and unrealities in which crime entangles ambition, the thousand-eyed genius of wilful error is smitten with folly and madness. No human intellect, however vast its compass and delicate its tact, can safely thread those terrible mazes. "Every heaven-stormer," says a quaint German, "finds his hell, as sure as every mountain its valley." Let us not doubt the genius of Washington because it was identical with wisdom, and because its energies worked with, and not against, the spiritual order its "single eye" was gifted to divine. We commonly say that he acted in accordance with moral laws; but we must recollect that moral laws are intellectual facts, and are known through intellectual processes. We commonly say that he was so conscientious as ever to follow the path of right, and obey the voice of duty. But what is right but an abstract term for rights? What is duty but an abstract term for duties? Rights and duties move not in parallel but converging lines; and how, in the terror, discord, and madness of a civil war, with rights and duties in confused conflict, can a man seize on the exact point where clashing rights harmonize, and where opposing duties are reconciled, and act vigorously on the conception, without having a conscience so informed with intelligence that his nature gravitates to the truth as by the very instinct and essence of reason?

The virtues of Washington, therefore, appear moral or mental according as we view them with the eye of conscience or reason. In him loftiness did not exclude breadth, but resulted from it; justice did not exclude wisdom, but grew out of it; and, as the wisest as well as justest man in America, he was preëminently distinguished among his contemporaries for moderation, — a word under which weak politicians conceal their want of courage, and knavish politicians their want of principle, but which in him was vital and comprehensive energy, tempering audacity with prudence, self-reliance with modesty, austere principles with merciful charities, inflexible purpose with serene courtesy, and issuing in that persistent and unconquerable fortitude, in which he excelled all mankind. In scrutinizing the events of his life to discover the processes by which his character grew gradually up to its amazing height, we are arrested at the beginning by the character of his mother, a woman temperate like him in the use of words, from her clear perception and vigorous grasp of things. There is a familiar anecdote recorded of her, which enables us to understand the simple sincerity and genuine heroism she early instilled into his strong and aspiring mind. At a time when his glory rang through Europe; when excitable enthusiasts were crossing the Atlantic for the single purpose of seeing him; when bad poets all over the world were sacking the dictionaries for hyperboles of panegyric; when the pedants of republicanism were calling him the American Cincinnatus and the American Fabius — as if our Washington were honored in playing the adjective to any Roman, however illustrious! — she, in her quiet dignity, simply said to the voluble friends who were striving to flatter her mother's pride into an expression of exulting praise, "that he had been a good son, and she believed he had done his duty as a man." Under the care of a mother, who flooded common words with such a wealth of meaning, the boy was not likely to mistake mediocrity for excellence, but would naturally domesticate in his heart lofty principles of conduct, and act from them as a matter of course, without expecting or obtaining praise. The consequence was, that in early life, and in his first occupation as surveyor, and through the stirring events of the French war, he built up character day by day in a systematic endurance of hardship; in a constant sacrifice of inclinations to duty; in taming hot passions into the service of reason; in assiduously learning from other minds; in wringing knowledge, which could not be taught him, from the reluctant grasp of a flinty experience; in completely mastering every subject on which he fastened his intellect, so that whatever he knew he knew perfectly and forever, transmuting it into mind, and sending it forth in acts. Intellectual and moral principles, which other men lazily contemplate and talk about, he had learned through a process which gave them the toughness of muscle and bone. A man thus sound at the core and on the surface of his nature; so full at once of integrity and sagacity; speaking ever from the level of his character, and always ready to substantiate opinions with deeds; — a man without any morbid egotism, or pretension, or extravagance; simple, modest, dignified, incorruptible; never giving advice which events did not endorse as wise, never lacking fortitude to bear calamities which resulted from his advice being overruled; — such a man could not but exact that recognition of commanding genius which inspires universal confidence. Accordingly, when the contest between the colonies and the mother country was assuming its inevitable form of civil war, he was found to be our natural leader in virtue of being the ablest man among a crowd of able men. When he appeared among the eloquent orators, the ingenious thinkers, the vehement patriots, of the revolution, his modesty and temperate professions could not conceal his superiority: he at once, by the very nature of great character, was felt to be their leader; towered up, indeed, over all their heads as naturally as the fountain, sparkling yonder in this July sun, which, in its long, dark, downward journey, forgets not the altitude of its parent lake, and no sooner finds an outlet in our lower lands than it mounts, by an impatient instinct, surely up to the level of its far-off inland source.

After the first flush and fever of the revolutionary excitement was over, and the haggard fact of civil war was visible in all its horrors, it soon appeared how vitally important was such a character to the success of such a cause. We have already seen that the issue of the contest depended, not on the decision of this or that battle, not on the occupation of this or that city, but on the power of the colonists to wear out the patience, exhaust the resources, and tame the pride of Great Britain. The king, when Lord North threatened, in 1778, to resign unless the war were discontinued, expressed his determination to lose his crown rather than acknowledge the independence of the rebels; he was as much opposed to that acknowledgment in 1783 as 1778; and it was only by a pressure from without, and when the expenditures for the war had reached a hundred million of pounds, that a reluctant consent was forced from that small, spiteful mind. Now, there was undoubtedly a vast majority of the American people unalterably resolved on independence; but they were spread through thirteen colonies, were not without mutual jealousies, and were represented in a Congress whose delegated powers were insufficient to prosecute war with vigor. The problem was, how to combine the strength, allay the suspicions, and sustain the patriotism of the people, during a contest peculiarly calculated to distract and weaken their energies. Washington solved this problem by the true geometry of indomitable personal character. He was the soul of the revolution, felt at its centre, and felt through all its parts, as an uniting, organizing, animating power. Comprehensive as America itself, through him, and through him alone, could the strength of America act. He was security in defeat, cheer in despondency, light in darkness, hope in despair — the one man in whom all could have confidence — the one man whose sun-like integrity and capacity shot rays of light and heat through everything they shone upon. He would not stoop to thwart the machinations of envy; he would not stoop to contradict the fictions and forgeries of calumny; and he did not need to do it. Before the effortless might of his character, they stole away, and withered, and died; and through no instrumentality of his did their abject authors become immortal as the maligners of Washington.

To do justice to Washington's military career, we must consider that he had to fuse the hardest individual materials into a mass of national force, which was to do battle, not only with disciplined armies, but with frost, famine, and disease. Missing the rapid succession of brilliant engagements between forces almost equal, and the dramatic storm and swift consummation of events, which European campaigns have made familiar, there are those who see in him only a slow, sure, and patient commander, without readiness of combination or energy of movement. But the truth is, the quick eye of his prudent audacity seized occasions to deliver blows with the prompt felicity of Marlborough or Wellington. He evinced no lack of the highest energy and skill when he turned back the tide of defeat at Monmouth, or in the combinations which preceded the siege of Yorktown, or in the rapid and masterly movements by which, at a period when he was considered utterly ruined, he stooped suddenly down upon Trenton, broke up all the enemy's posts on the Delaware, and snatched Philadelphia from a superior and victorious foe. Again, some eulogists have caricatured him as a passionless, imperturbable, "proper" man; but, at the battle of Monmouth, General Lee was privileged to discover, that from those firm, calm lips could leap words hotter and more smiting than the hot June sun that smote down upon their heads. Indeed, Washington's incessant and various activity answered to the strange complexity of his position, as the heart and brain of a revolution, which demanded not merely generalship, but the highest qualities of the statesman, the diplomatist, and the patriot. As we view him in his long seven years' struggle with the perilous difficulties of his situation, his activity constantly entangled in a mesh of conflicting considerations, — with his eye fixed on Congress, on the States, and on the people, as well as on the enemy, — compelled to compose sectional quarrels, to inspire faltering patriotism, and to triumph over all the forces of stupidity and selfishness, — compelled to watch, and wait, and warn, and forbear, and endure, as well as to act, — compelled, amid vexations and calamities which would sting the dullest sensibilities into madness, to transmute the fire of the fiercest passion into an element of fortitude; — and, especially, as we view him coming out of that terrible and obscure scene of trial and temptation, without any bitterness in his virtue, or hatred in his patriotism, but full of the loftiest wisdom and serenest power; — as we view all this in the order of its history, that placid face grows gradually sublime, and in its immortal repose looks rebuke to our presumptuous eulogium of the genius which breathes through it!

We all know that towards the end of the wearying struggle, and when his matchless moderation and invincible fortitude were about to be crowned with the hallowing glory which Liberty piously reserves for her triumphant saints and martyrs, a committee of his officers proposed to make him king; and we sometimes do him the cruel injustice to say that his virtue overcame the *temptation*. He was not knave enough, or fool enough, to be tempted by such criminal baubles. What was his view of the proposal? He who had never sought popularity, but whom popularity had sought, — he who had entered public life, not for the pleasure of exercising power, but for the satisfaction of performing duty, — he to be insulted and outraged by such an estimate of his services, and such a conception of his character! — why, it could provoke in him nothing but an instantaneous burst of indignation and abhorrence! — and, in his reply, you will find that these emotions strain the language of reproof beyond the stern courtesy of military decorum.

The war ended, and our independence acknowledged, the time came when American liberty, threatened by anarchy, was to be re-organized in the Constitution of the United States. As President of the Convention which framed the Constitution, Washington powerfully contributed to its acceptance by the States. The people were uncertain as to the equity of its compromise of opposing interests, and adjustment of clashing claims. By this eloquent and learned man they were advised to adopt it; by that eloquent and learned man they were advised to reject it; but there, at the end of the instrument itself, and first among many eminent and honored names, was the bold and honest signature of George Washington, a signature which always carried with it the integrity and the influence of his character; and that was an argument stronger even than any furnished by Hamilton, Madison, and Jay. The Constitution was accepted; and Washington, whose fame, to use Allston's familiar metaphor, was ever the shadow cast by his excellence, was of course unanimously elected President. This is no place to set forth the glories of his civil career. It is sufficient to say that placed amid circumstances where ignorance, vanity, or rashness would have worked ruinous mischief and disunion, he consolidated the government. One little record in his diary, just before he entered upon his office, is a key to the spirit of his administration. His journey from Mount Vernon to the seat of government was a triumphal procession. At New York the air was alive with that tumult of popular applause, which has poisoned the integrity by intoxicating the pride of so many eminent generals and statesmen. What was the feeling of Washington? Did he have a misanthrope's cynical contempt for the people's honest tribute of gratitude? Did he have a demagogue's fierce elation in being the object of the people's boundless admiration? No. His sensations, he tells us, were as painful as they were pleasing. His lofty and tranquil mind thought of the possible reverse of the scene after all his exertions to do good. The streaming flags, the loud acclamations, the thunder of the cannon, and the shrill music piercing through all other sounds, — these sent his mind sadly forward to the solitude of his closet, where, with the tender and beautiful austerity of his character, he was perhaps to sacrifice the people's favor for the people's safety, and to employ every granted power of a constitution he so perfectly understood, in preserving peace, in restraining faction, and in giving energy to all those constitutional restraints on popular passions, by which the wisdom of to-morrow rules the recklessness of to-day.

In reviewing a life thus passed in enduring hardship and confronting peril, fretted by constant cares and worn by incessant drudgery, we are at first saddened by the thought that such heroic virtue should have been purchased by the sacrifice of happiness. But we wrong Washington in bringing his enjoyments to the test of our low standards. He has everything for us to venerate — nothing for our commiseration.

He tasted of that joy which springs from a sense of great responsibilities willingly incurred, and great duties magnanimously performed. To him was given the deep bliss of seeing the austere countenance of inexorable Duty melt into approving smiles, and to him was realized the poet's rapturous vision of her celestial compensations: —

"Stern Lawgiver! yet thou dost wear
The Godhead's most benignant grace,
Nor know we anything so fair
As is the smile upon thy face."

It has been truly said that "men of intemperate minds cannot be free; their passions forge their fetters;" but no clank of any chain, whether of avarice or ambition, gave the least harshness to the movement of Washington's ample mind. In him America has produced at least one man, whose free soul was fit to be Liberty's chosen home. As was his individual freedom, so should be our national freedom. We have seen all along, that American liberty, in its sentiment and idea, is no opinionated, will-strong, untamable passion, bursting all bounds of moral restraint, and hungering after anarchy and license, but a creative and beneficent energy, organizing itself in laws, professions, trades, arts, institutions. From its extreme practical character, however, it is liable to contract a taint which has long vitiated English freedom. To the Anglo-Saxon mind, Liberty is not apt to be the enthusiast's mountain nymph, with cheeks wet with morning dew and clear eyes that mirror the heavens, but rather is she an old dowager lady, fatly invested in commerce and manufactures, and peevishly fearful that enthusiasm will reduce her establishment, and panics cut off her dividends. Now the moment property becomes timid, agrarianism becomes bold; and the industry which liberty has created, liberty must animate, or it will be plundered by the impudent and rapacious idleness its slavish fears incite. Our political institutions, again, are but the body of which liberty is the soul; their preservation depends on their being continually inspired by the light and heat of the sentiment and idea whence they sprung; and when we timorously suspend, according to the latest political fashion, the truest and dearest maxims of our freedom at the call of expediency or the threat of passion, — when we convert politics into a mere game of interests, unhallowed by a single great and unselfish principle, — we may be sure that our worst passions are busy "forging our fetters;" that we are proposing all those intricate problems which red republicanism so swiftly solves, and giving Manifest Destiny pertinent hints to shout new anthems of atheism over victorious rapine. The liberty which our fathers planted, and for which they sturdily contended, and under which they grandly conquered, is a rational and temperate but brave and unyielding freedom, the august mother of institutions, the hardy nurse of enterprise, the sworn ally of justice and order; a Liberty that lifts her awful and rebuking face equally upon the cowards who would sell, and the braggarts who would pervert, her precious gifts of rights and obligations; and this Liberty we are solemnly bound at all hazards to protect, at any sacrifice to preserve, and by all just means to extend, against the unbridled excesses of that ugly and brazen hag, originally scorned and detested by those who unwisely gave her infancy a home, but which now, in her enormous growth and favored deformity, reels with blood-shot eyes, and dishevelled tresses, and words of unshamed slavishness, into halls where Liberty should sit throned!

www.ingramcontent.com/pod-product-compliance
Lightning Source LLC
LaVergne TN
LVHW050543100826
845148LV00002B/666
* 9 7 8 1 4 2 5 5 7 5 9 3 9 *